See and Say
Arabic

by Susan Muaddi Darraj

PEBBLE
a capstone imprint

Published by Pebble, an imprint of Capstone
1710 Roe Crest Drive, North Mankato, Minnesota 56003
capstonepub.com

Copyright © 2025 by Capstone. All rights reserved. No part of this publication may be reproduced in whole or in part, or stored in a retrieval system, or transmitted in any form or by any means, electronic, mechanical, photocopying, recording, or otherwise, without written permission of the publisher.

Library of Congress Cataloging-in-Publication Data is available on the Library of Congress website.
ISBN: 9780756587338 (hardcover)
ISBN: 9780756587284 (paperback)
ISBN: 9780756587291 (ebook PDF)

Summary: How do you ask nicely for something in Arabic? What's the Arabic word for *shoes*? With this book, curious kids will see and say simple words and phrases in Arabic.

Editorial Credits
Editor: Ericka Smith; Designer: Sarah Bennett; Media Researcher: Svetlana Zhurkin; Production Specialist: Katy LaVigne

Image Credits
Alamy: Janine Wiedel Photolibrary, 18 (bottom right), Jeremy Graham, 19 (top right), Zuma Wire/APA Images/Muammar Awad, 26 (bottom); Dreamstime: Alan Gignoux, 20 (middle), Sarit Richerson, 12 (top right), Wirestock, 13 (middle right), 25 (bottom left); Getty Images: AFP/Ramzi Haidar, 23 (bottom), Ahmed Zakot, 22 (middle left), armankose, 22 (bottom), Bruce Laurance, 23 (top right), JohnnyGreig, 7 (top), 9 (top), Juanmonlno, 23 (middle left), lenazap, 11 (top right), Maskot, 14 (top), Master, 14 (middle), Nick Brundle Photography, 4, onfilm, 21 (bottom right), ozgurdonmaz, 7 (bottom right), 16 (top), TonySamia, 25 (top left), VvoeVale, 26 (top left); Shutterstock: 3ffi, 10 (top right), Aleksandr Sadkov, 19 (bottom), Ali Mahmoud Zaher, 25 (bottom right), Anna Om, 5 (bottom), 6, 25 (top right), AS Foodstudio, 10 (middle), asife, 31 (middle), bergamont, 29 (middle right), Boonchuay Promjiam, 29 (bottom left), daniiD, 17 (bottom left), Denis Esaulov 1987, 11 (bottom), EcoPrint, 13 (bottom), Elizabeth_0102, 29 (middle left), Eric Isselee, 13 (top right, middle left), ESB Professional, 19 (top left), FamVeld, 30 (middle left), Fascinadora, 30 (middle), Fotofermer, 28 (bottom left), Fotokon, 18 (bottom left), gan chaonan, 12 (top left), Georgios Tsichlis, 19 (middle), GeptaYs, 12 (bottom right), halimqd (speech bubble and burst), cover and throughout, Hashem Issam Alshanableh, 10 (bottom), Henner Damke, 13 (top left), Irina Wilhauk, 31 (top), Kamil Al Rayess, 18 (middle), koss13, 10 (top left), Ladanifer, 23 (top left), leshiy985, 18 (top), 21 (middle), Lily81, 27 (top), Magnia (lined texture), cover and throughout, MalikNalik, 9 (bottom), Markus Mainka, 21 (top), Maryna Osadcha, 11 (middle right), MidoSemsem, 7 (bottom left), Moatassem, 26 (top right), Momen_frames, 15 (top), Monkey Business Images, 8, Naypong Studio, 29 (top), New Africa, 17 (middle left), nukeaf, 24, oksana2010, 28 (top right), Omar Al-Hyari, 20 (bottom), Photoongraphy, cover (top right), Pixel-Shot, cover (top left), 22 (top), Prostock-studio, 7 (middle), 14 (bottom), 15 (middle), 23 (middle right), Rahhal, cover (bottom right), 1, Rich Carey, cover (bottom left), Ruth Black, 30 (top, middle right, bottom), 31 (middle right, middle left, bottom), Sergey Novikov, 16 (bottom), Sergey-73, 20 (top), Sergiy1975, cover (middle left), spiharu.u (spot line art), cover and throughout, Stewart Innes, 11 (bread), stockphoto mania, 12 (bottom left), Sun_Shine, 21 (bottom left), Tim UR, 28 (top left), Vangert, 28 (bottom right), Vlad Teodor, 17 (top), webwaffe, 11 (middle left), winphong, 29 (bottom right), Wirestock Creators, 27 (bottom), yampi, 15 (bottom), Zeid AbuSaad, 11 (top left), ZouZou, 17 (middle right), Zurijeta, 5 (top), 22 (middle right)

Any additional websites and resources referenced in this book are not maintained, authorized, or sponsored by Capstone. All product and company names are trademarks™ or registered® trademarks of their respective holders.

Printed in the United States   6310

Table of Contents

The Arabic Language.............................. 4

Greetings and Phrases........................... 6

Family.. 8

Food... 10

Animals... 12

At Home... 14

Clothing 16

In the Neighborhood 18

Transportation 20

Hobbies 22

Days of the Week 24

Seasons 25

Weather 26

Colors... 28

Numbers.. 30

About the Translator 32

The Arabic Language

Arabic is 2,500 years old. Today, more than 400 million people speak Arabic. In Arabic-speaking countries, the official language is Modern Standard Arabic. It's used in things like newspapers, magazines, and contracts. But most people speak a particular dialect—or form—of Arabic. This book covers the Levantine (lehv-UHN-tahyn) dialect. It is popular in Lebanon, Palestine, Jordan, and Syria.

An official language is a language that many people in a country speak. It might be used by the government, at schools, and in other important places.

How to Use This Book

Some words and phrases complete a sentence. Those will appear in bold.

English	I like . . .
Arabic	انا بحب
Say It! 🐱	ah-nah bah-hib

+

English	reading.
Arabic	قرأة
Say It! 🐱	kir-ah

Others give you the name for a person, place, thing, or idea.

English	spring
Arabic	ربيع
Say It! 🐱	al-rah-bee

Read Right to Left
Arabic is a language that you read from right to left—the opposite direction of English!

Meet Chatty Cat! Chatty Cat will show you how to say the words and phrases in this book.

Masculine and Feminine Words
In Arabic, some nouns have a masculine and feminine form. For example, you'd use a different word for *doctor* depending on whether the doctor is a woman or a man. But you can also use the masculine form when speaking generally. In this book, you'll see the masculine form of a word.

Greetings and Phrases

Arabic تَحِيَّات
Say It! tah-hee-yat

English Hello!
Arabic مَرحَبا
Say It! mar-hah-bah

English My name is . . .
Arabic اسمي
Say It! iss-mee

English What is your name?
Arabic شو إسمك؟
Say It! iss-mak shoo

English How are you?
Arabic كيفَك؟
Say It! kee-fak

English I am fine.
Arabic أنا بخير
Say It! an-nah bi-khayr

Kh in Arabic

The letters *kh* represent an *h* sound that you use more of your throat to pronounce. It should sound a little like you're trying to clear something stuck in your throat.

English Nice to meet you.
Arabic فرصة سعيدة
Say It! fur-sa saa-ee-dah

English	Please.
Arabic	من فضلك
Say It!	min-fad-lak

English	Thank you!
Arabic	شكراً
Say It!	shuk-run

English	You're welcome!
Arabic	عفوا
Say It!	aaf-wan

English	Goodbye!
Arabic	مع السلامة
Say It!	ma-aa-sah-lah-mah

English	See you later!
Arabic	بشوفك
Say It!	bah-shoo-fak

English	Yes.
Arabic	نعم
Say It!	nah-aam

English	No.
Arabic	لا
Say It!	lah

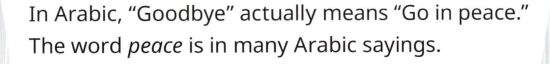

In Arabic, "Goodbye" actually means "Go in peace." The word *peace* is in many Arabic sayings.

Family

Arabic	عيلة
Say It!	aay-leh

English	This is . . .
Arabic	هذا (boy speaking)
Say It!	hah-thah
Arabic	هذي (girl speaking)
Say It!	hah-thee

English	my father.
Arabic	أبوي
Say It!	ah-boi-ee

English	my mother.
Arabic	أمي
Say It!	im-mee

English	my sister.
Arabic	أختي
Say It!	ukh-tee

English	my brother.
Arabic	أخوي
Say It!	ah-khoo-yee

English my grandfather.
Arabic جدي
Say It! jid-dee

English my grandmother.
Arabic جدتي
Say It! jid-det-tee

English my aunt.
Arabic عمتي (father's side)
Say It! aam-tee
Arabic خالتي (mother's side)
Say It! khal-tee

English my uncle.
Arabic عمّي (father's side)
Say It! aam-mee
Arabic خالي (mother's side)
Say It! khal-lee

English my cousin.
Arabic ابن عمّي (boy, father's side)
Say It! ib-in-aam-mee
Arabic ابن خالي (boy, mother's side)
Say It! ib-in-khal-tee
Arabic بنت عمّي (girl, father's side)
Say It! bint aam-mee
Arabic بنت خالي (girl, mother's side)
Say It! bint khal-tee

In Arab families, you refer to your aunts, uncles, and cousins differently depending on whether they are related to your mother or father.

9

Food

Arabic طعام
Say It! tah-aam

English I'm hungry. I want . . .
Arabic انا جوعان بدي (boy speaking)
Say It! an-nah joo-aan bid-dee
Arabic انا جوعانه بدي (girl speaking)
Say It! an-nah joo-aan-eh bid-dee

English breakfast.
Arabic إفطار
Say It! if-tar

English hummus
Arabic حمّص
Say It! hum-muss

English labneh
Arabic لبنة
Say It! lab-neh

English lunch.
Arabic غداء
Say It! gha-daa

English falafel
Arabic فلافل
Say It! fah-lah-fil

English shawarmah
Arabic شاورما
Say It! shah-wir-mah

Gh in Arabic

The letters *gh* represent a sound similar to *kh*. You use more of your throat to pronounce it. It should sound a little like gargling and like saying the letter *r*.

English	dinner.
Arabic	عشاء
Say It! 🐱	aa-shah

English	maqloubeh
Arabic	مقلوبة
Say It! 🐱	mek-loo-beh

English	mansaff
Arabic	منسف
Say It! 🐱	men-sef

English	a snack.
Arabic	لقمة
Say It! 🐱	look-meh

English	bread
Arabic	خبز
Say It! 🐱	khu-bihz

English	cucumber
Arabic	خيار
Say It! 🐱	khee-yahr

English	pomegranate
Arabic	رمان
Say It! 🐱	room-mahn

English	milk
Arabic	حليب
Say It! 🐱	hah-leeb

Maqloubeh means "upside down" in Arabic. Maqloubeh is a popular dish of rice and meat that has been cooked in a pot and flipped over onto a serving platter.

11

Animals

Arabic حيوانات

Say It! 🐱 hay-wah-naht

English a camel
Arabic جمل
Say It! 🐱 ja-mel

English a dog
Arabic كلب
Say It! 🐱 keh-lib

English a horse
Arabic حصان
Say It! 🐱 ha-sahn

English a chicken
Arabic دجاج
Say It! 🐱 dej-jahj

English a fish
Arabic سمك
Say It! sah-mahk

English a lamb
Arabic غنم
Say It! ghah-nehm

English a cat
Arabic قطة
Say It! kuh-tah

English a bird
Arabic عصفور
Say It! aas-foor

English a gazelle
Arabic غزال
Say It! ghah-zahl

13

At Home

Arabic في البيت
Say It! fee al-bayt

English kitchen
Arabic مطبخ
Say It! muht-bukh

English table
Arabic طاولة
Say It! taw-leh

English chair
Arabic كرسي
Say It! kuhr-see

English living room
Arabic أوضة القعدة
Say It! aw-dah al-kaa-deh

English couch
Arabic كنباية
Say It! kah-nah-bah-yeh

English door
Arabic باب
Say It! bab

English computer
Arabic كومبيوتر
Say It! kuhm-byoo-tuhr

14

English bedroom
Arabic أوضة النوم
Say It! aw-dah al-nohm

English bed
Arabic تخت
Say It! tah-khet

English cell phone
Arabic تلفون موبيل
Say It! te-le-foon moh-beel

English window
Arabic شبّاك
Say It! shuh-bak

English bathroom
Arabic حمّام
Say It! ham-maam

English bathtub
Arabic حوض
Say It! haw-dh

English toilet
Arabic مرحاض
Say It! mer-badh

English sink
Arabic مغسلة
Say It! magh-sah-leh

There are some letters in English that do not exist in Arabic, like *p* and *v*. Arabic speakers sometimes use the sound of *b* for these letters.

15

Clothing

Arabic	ملابس
Say It!	melah-biss

> | English | I am wearing . . . |
> |---|---|
> | Arabic | أنا لابس (boy) |
> | Say It! | an-nah lah-biss |
> | Arabic | أنا لابسه (girl) |
> | Say It! | an-nah lab-seh |

English	a shirt.
Arabic	قميص
Say It!	kah-mees

English	a hat.
Arabic	طاقيّة
Say It!	tah-kee-yeh

English	a coat.
Arabic	كبّوت
Say It!	kah-boot

English	pants.
Arabic	بنطلون
Say It!	bun-tah-lown

16

English a skirt.
Arabic تنّورة
Say It! tuh-noo-rah

English hijab.
Arabic حجاب
Say It! hi-jahb

English socks.
Arabic كلسات
Say It! kel-saht

English shoes.
Arabic كنادر
Say It! keh-nah-dir

English a dress.
Arabic فستان
Say It! foos-tahn

17

In the Neighborhood

Arabic مِنْطَقة في ال
Say It! fee al mon-tee-kah

English a street
Arabic شارع
Say It! shah-raa

English a house
Arabic بيت
Say It! bayt

English a hospital
Arabic مستشفى
Say It! mus-tesh-fah

English a school
Arabic مدرسة
Say It! med-rah-sah

18

English	a library
Arabic	مكتبة
Say It!	mek-tah-bah

English	a post office
Arabic	مكتب البريد
Say It!	mak-teb al-bah-reed

English	a mosque
Arabic	مسجد
Say It!	mas-jid

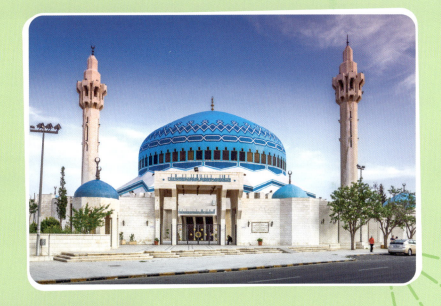

English	a church
Arabic	كنيسة
Say It!	kah-nee-seh

19

Transportation

Arabic مواصلات
Say It! mu-ah-sah-laht

English a boat
Arabic سفينة
Say It! sah-fee-neh

English a bus
Arabic باص
Say It! baas

English a bicycle
Arabic بسكليت
Say It! bes-kel-ayt

English an airplane
Arabic طائرة
Say It! tay-irah

English a car
Arabic سيارة
Say It! see-yah-rah

English a truck
Arabic شاحنة
Say It! sha-hee-nah

English a train
Arabic قطار
Say It! kee-tar

Hobbies

Arabic هوايات
Say It! hee-wah-yat

English I like . . .
Arabic انا بحب
Say It! ah-nah ba-hib

English singing.
Arabic الغناء
Say It! al-ghee-nah

English reading.
Arabic قرأة
Say It! kir-ah

English embroidery.
Arabic تطريز
Say It! tat-reez

English a book
Arabic كتاب
Say It! ki-taab

English backgammon.
Arabic طاولة الزهر
Say It! taw-let al-zah-hir

22

English soccer.
Arabic كرة القدم
Say It! koo-rat al-kah-dim

English a ball
Arabic طابة
Say It! taa-beh

English basketball.
Arabic كرة السلة
Say It! koo-rat ah-sel-eh

English swimming.
Arabic سباحة
Say It! see-bah-hah

English cooking.
Arabic طبخ
Say It! tahb-akh

English line dancing.
Arabic دبكة
Say It! deb-kah

Days of the Week

Arabic	أيام الأسبوع
Say It!	ay-yam al-as-boo-aa

> | English | Today is . . . |
> |---|---|
> | Arabic | اليوم هوا |
> | Say It! | al-youm how-wah |

English	Monday.
Arabic	الإثْنَين
Say It!	al-ith-nayn

English	Tuesday.
Arabic	الثَلاثاء
Say It!	al-thal-ah-thah

English	Wednesday.
Arabic	الأربَعاء
Say It!	al-ar-bah-aa

English	Thursday.
Arabic	الخَميس
Say It!	al-khah-mees

English	Friday.
Arabic	الجُمُعة
Say It!	al-jum-aa

English	Saturday.
Arabic	السَبْت
Say It!	al-sabt

English	Sunday.
Arabic	الأحَد
Say It!	al-ah-hed

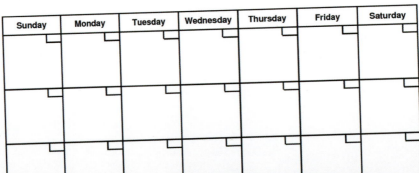

Seasons

Arabic مواسم
Say It! mah-wah-sim

English winter
Arabic شتاء
Say It! shih-teh

English spring
Arabic ربيع
Say It! al-rah-bee

English summer
Arabic صيف
Say It! sayf

English fall
Arabic خريف
Say It! kha-reef

Weather

Arabic طقس
Say It! tahks

English It is windy.
Arabic عاصف
Say It! aa-sif

English It is raining.
Arabic إنها تمطر
Say It! in-nah-hah tah-mat-tar

English It is cold.
Arabic الطقس بارد
Say It! ah-tahks baa-rid

English It is snowing.
Arabic إنها تثلج
Say It! in-nah-hah tet-lij

English It is hot.
Arabic الجو حار
Say It! al-jow har

English It is sunny.
Arabic يوم مشمس
Say It! youm muh-shah-miss

English It is cloudy.
Arabic يوم مغيم
Say It! youm muh-ghay-ahm

27

Colors

Arabic الألوان
Say It! al al-wahn

English red
Arabic أحمر
Say It! ah-mahr

English pink
Arabic وردي
Say It! war-dee

English green
Arabic أخضر
Say It! akh-dar

English orange
Arabic برتقالي
Say It! bur-too-kah-lee

English blue
Arabic أزرق
Say It! az-rahk

English yellow
Arabic أصفر
Say It! as-faar

English purple
Arabic البَنفِسِجي
Say It! al-ben-fes-jee

English black
Arabic أسود
Say It! ess-wed

English white
Arabic أبيض
Say It! ab-yahd

29

Numbers

Arabic الارقام
Say It! al-ar-kahm

1
English one
Arabic واحد
Say It! wah-hed

2
English two
Arabic إثنان
Say It! ith-nayn

3
English three
Arabic ثلاثة
Say It! tha-lah-thah

4
English four
Arabic أربعة
Say It! ar-baa-ah

5
English five
Arabic خمسة
Say It! kham-seh

6
English six
Arabic ستة
Say It! 🐱 sit-teh

7
English seven
Arabic سبعة
Say It! 🐱 seb-ah

8
English eight
Arabic ثمانية
Say It! 🐱 thah-men-yeh

9
English nine
Arabic تسعة
Say It! 🐱 tiss-aa

10
English ten
Arabic عشرة
Say It! 🐱 aa-shah-rah

About the Translator

Susan Muaddi Darraj is an award-winning writer for adults and children. She is the author of the Farah Rocks chapter books, the first book series to feature a Palestinian American character. She is the recipient of an American Book Award, a Ford Fellowship, and two Arab American Book Awards. Her latest novel, *Behind You Is the Sea*, was published in 2024 by HarperCollins.